THE ULTIMATE DAD JOKE BOOK

THAT'S SO DAD

Are monsters good at math?
Not unless you count Dracula.

KID: "Dad, you can always store your photos on the cloud."
DAD: "But what if it's sunny?"

What's a tornado's favorite game?
Twister!

If at first you don't succeed, skydiving is not for you!

Why should you never tell a pig your secret?
Because it is sure to squeal.

What's the difference between a pickpocket and an umpire?
One steals watches and one watches steals.

Why did the turkey cross the road?
To prove he wasn't chicken.

How does a hurricane see?
With one eye.

I keep trying to lose weight, but it keeps finding me.

Why were the utensils stuck together? They were spooning.

What did the limestone say to the geologist? Don't take me for granite.

I knew I shouldn't steal a mixer from work, but it was a whisk I was willing to take.

3

What do porcupines say when they kiss?
Ouch!

I'm on a whiskey diet. I've lost three days already.

What do you call it when a prisoner takes his own mugshot?
A cellfie.

Shout-out to my grandma; that's the only way she can hear.

I sliced my finger when cutting fruit! Now we have blood oranges!

Why does Dad not take soccer seriously? Because he's just doing it for the kicks.

I spent a lot of time, money and effort child proofing my house... but the kids still get in.

Do you wanna box for your leftovers? No, but I'll wrestle you for them.

How do you get a farm girl to like you?
A tractor.

Archaeology really is a career in ruins.

Why is it bad idea to insult an octopus?
Because they are well-armed.

Why does the baker go to work?
Because he kneads the dough.

The rotation of the Earth really make my day.

How did they get the confession out of the hamburger? They grilled him.

Will these portabellas fit in the fridge? I don't know if there's mushroom left.

I was going to tell a time-traveling joke, but you didn't like it.

Chances are if you've seen one shopping center, you've seen a mall.

Could you please open the jam container?
Why? It's already a jar.

My doctor told me I'm going deaf.
The news was hard for me to hear.

What did the pirate say on his 80th birthday?
"AYE MATEY"

What do you call a white bucket?
Pail.

Why was the strawberry late?
He was caught in a jam.

Do you know why I got fired from the calendar factory?
Because I took a couple of days off.

I went to the zoo and saw a piece of toast in a cage. The sign said, "bread in captivity."

Chances are if you've seen one shopping center, you've seen a mall.

Could you please open the jam container?
Why? It's already a jar.

My doctor told me I'm going deaf.
The news was hard for me to hear.

What did the pirate say on his 80th birthday?
"AYE MATEY"

8

What do you call a white bucket?
Pail.

Why was the strawberry late?
He was caught in a jam.

Do you know why I got fired from the calendar factory?
Because I took a couple of days off.

I went to the zoo and saw a piece of toast in a cage. The sign said, "bread in captivity."

What is the leading cause of dry skin?
Towels.

Never date a tennis player. Love means nothing to them.

For Valentine's Day I decided to get my wife some beads for an abacus. It's the little things that count.

MOM:
"How do I look?"
DAD:
"With your eyes!"

There's dog hair all over the house. We should call it a shed.

Why couldn't the lifeguard save the hippie?
He was too far out, man.

Can a kangaroo jump higher than the Empire State Building?
Of course! Buildings can't jump.

What has to be broken before you can use it?
An egg.

> I finally watched that documentary on clocks. It was about time.

> What type of medicine do ants use when they have eye problems? Ant-eye-biotics.

> My teacher said that if I spilled coffee, it would be grounds for suspension!

> A cheese factory exploded in France, da brie is everywhere!

What has more letters than the alphabet?
The post office!

Why did the calendar seem so popular?
Because it had a lot of dates!

What happens when the smog lifts in Southern California?
UCLA.

What do you call a blind deer?
No ideer.

My boss told me to have a good day, so I went home.

What is Beethoven's favorite fruit?
A ba-na-na-na.

I was going to get a brain transplant, but I changed my mind.

Did you hear the one about the guy with the broken hearing aid?
Neither did he.

What kind of music do mummies love? Wrap music.

Why is the lunch meat on the floor? Because it's below knee.

What did the daddy tomato say to the baby tomato? Catch up!

I could never be a plumber. It's too hard watching your life's work go down the drain.

Doctor: "I think your DNA is backwards."
Me: "AND?"

If you see a robbery at an apple store does that make you an iWitness?

Last night me and my wife watched three DVDs back to back. Luckily I was the one facing the TV.

Why did the dad take a while to decide on a haircut?
Because he had to mullet over.

Politics are ridiculous, but do you know what truly is backwards?
Ylurt

Why is it a bad idea to iron your four-leaf clover?
Because you shouldn't press your luck.

I am terrified of elevators. I'm going to start taking steps to avoid them.

Why did the student eat his homework?
Because his teacher told him it would be a piece of cake!

Why do melons have weddings?
Because they cantaloupe.

Why should you never buy anything with Velcro?
Because it's a total rip-off!

Swords will never become obsolete. They're cutting-edge technology.

What do a tick and the Eiffel Tower have in common?
They're both Paris-sites.

How was the candle party?
It was lit!

People are usually shocked that I have a Police record.
But I love their greatest hits!

How did they fix the pirate's injured eye?
They patched it up.

Where do you go to make dessert?
To sundae school.

Why couldn't the couple get married at the library? It was all booked up.

Without geometry life is pointless.

What is the worst part of a money addiction? Withdrawal.

Why did the banana put on sunscreen? Because he didn't want to peel!

Where do immortal college students shop? Forever 21.

What country's capital is growing the fastest? Ireland. Every day it's Dublin.

Sometimes I tuck my knees into my chest and lean forward. That's just how I roll.

How many apples grow in a tree? All of them.

Why was the student's report card wet?
It was below "C" level!

I gave all my dead batteries away today. Free of charge.

Did you know the first French fries were not actually cooked in France?
They were cooked in Greece.

I ordered a chicken and an egg from Amazon.
I'll let you know.

What do you call a man named David without an ID?
Dav.

Man, I love my furniture. Me and my recliner go way back.

What has four wheels and flies?
A garbage truck.

Why is "dark" spelled with a "k" and not a "c"?
Because you can't "c" the dark.

Why don't pirates take a bath before they walk the plank? They wash up onshore.

Why did the Energizer Bunny go to jail? He was charged with battery.

Why did the Easter Bunny study all night? He had an eggxam the next day.

My friend keeps saying "Cheer up man, it could be worse, you could be stuck underground in a hole full of water." I know he means well.

My friend said to me: "What rhymes with orange."
I said:
"No it doesn't."

I have a joke about a broken clock, but it's not the right time.

My son is studying to be a surgeon. I just hope he makes the cut.

Who oversees all the tissues?
The handkerchief.

What noise does a 747 make when it bounces?
Boeing, boeing, boeing.

Son: "Dad, did you get a haircut?"
Dad: "No, I got them all cut!"

What do you call someone with no body and no nose?
Nobody knows.

Rest in peace, boiled water.
You will be mist.

Did I tell you about the time I worked in a shoe recycling shop? It was sole destroying.

Why do you never see elephants hiding in trees? Because they're so good at it.

What do you call a funny mountain? Hill-arious.

How do you make sure the sea creature is playing the right song? You have to tuna fish.

Why is it hard to understand volunteers? Because they make no cents.

My wife told me I had to stop acting like a flamingo. So I had to put my foot down!

The guy at the seafood shop is so greedy. I'd go as far as to call him shellfish.

The bathroom sink is red because my mom colored her hair. It looks like someone dyed in there.

I'm attaching a light to the ceiling, but I'm afraid I'll screw it up.

What is the loudest pet there is?
A trumpet.

I went to buy some camouflage trousers the other day, but I couldn't find any.

Why are basketball players messy eaters?
Because they are always dribbling.

Why did the slug call the police?
Because it was a-salted.

What rock group has four men who don't sing?
Mount Rushmore.

What has one head, one foot, and four legs?
A bed.

Why did the mathematician get fat?
Because he ate too much pi.

What is the name of the fattest knight?
Sir Cumference.

Why does Sherlock Holmes love Mexican restaurants?
They give him good case ideas.

When do doctors get angry?
When they run out of patients.

Why did the golfer patch his pants?
Because he got a hole in one.

Americans can't switch from pounds to kilograms overnight. That would cause mass confusion.

The wedding I went to was so touching. Even the cake was in tiers!

Want to know why nurses like red crayons? Sometimes they have to draw blood.

Why did the burglar hang his mug shot on the wall?
To prove that he was framed!

What kind of underwear did Muhammed Ali wear?
Boxers!

Why did the triangle feel sorry for the circle?
Because it was pointless!

Why was the barber disqualified after winning the race?
He took a shortcut.

Why did the cookie cry?
Because his father was a wafer so long!

You got hit by a rental car?
Yeah, it Hertz.

Why did the invisible man turn down the job offer?
He couldn't see himself doing it.

What do dogs eat for breakfast?
Woofles.

Why was the big cat disqualified from the race?
Because it was a cheetah.

What did the vegetarian zombie say? "GRAAAIIIIIINS!"

I burnt my Hawaiian pizza today.
I should have set the oven to aloha temperature.

Why was it called the Dark Ages?
Because of all the knights.

A man got hit in the head with a can of soda.
He's alright though – it was a soft drink.

If your nose runs and your feet smell, you are built upside down!

Yesterday I was washing the car with my son. He said, "Dad, can't you just use a sponge?"

Did you hear about the carrot detective? He got to the root of every case.

Did I tell you the time I fell in love during a backflip? I was heels over head.

How do you get straight A's?
By using a ruler.

How many months have 28 days?
All of them!

What did the ocean say to the beach?
Nothing, it just waved.

Where do animals go when their tails fall off?
To the retail store!

Yesterday, a clown held a door open for me.
I thought it was a nice jester.

Why do trees look suspicious on sunny days?
They just seem a little shady.

I was fired from the keyboard factory yesterday.
I wasn't putting in enough shifts.

How do you get a boat delivered?
You ship it.

What do you call a nondescript potato?
A common-tater.

What is an astronaut's favorite key on a computer keyboard?
The space bar!

Why do pancakes always win in baseball?
They have the best batter.

"Doctor, you've got to help me, I'm addicted to Twitter."
Doctor: "I don't follow you."

Did you hear about the kidnapping at school? It's okay. He woke up.

I tried to win a sun-tanning competition. But all I got was bronze.

I once had a turtle as a teacher. He tortoise well.

Did you hear about the square that got into a car accident? Now he's a rect-angle!

How do celebrities stay cool?
They have many fans.

I needed a password eight characters long so I picked Snow White and the Seven Dwarfs.

My teachers told me I'd never amount to anything because I procrastinate so much. I told them, "Just you wait!"

Why did the two hamburgers not get along?
Because they had beef.

What do dentists call their x-rays?
Tooth pics!

What's the difference between a pun and a dad joke?
Dad jokes are punnier.

How do you cut the sea in half?
With a seesaw!

I was offered a construction job in Egypt.
Turned out to be a pyramid scheme.

Why did the pencil cross the road?
It was lead!

Where is the best place to work if you only have one leg?
IHOP!

Linda broke her finger today.
On the other hand, she was completely fine.

My seasickness comes in waves.

What type of tree fits your hand?
A palm tree.

I went to a smoke shop only to discover it had been replaced by an apparel store.
Clothes, but no cigar.

What's a pirate's favorite letter?
You'd think it's "R", but it's actually the "C".

Don't trust atoms.
They make up everything!

Do mascara and lipstick ever argue? Sure, but then they makeup.

Stop looking for the perfect match; use a lighter.

Why was the coach yelling at a vending machine? He wanted his quarterback.

When you have a bladder infection, urine trouble.

45

Why should you not trust dermatologists? They make too many rash decisions.

I was in a grocery store when a man started to throw cheese, butter, and yogurt at me. How dairy!

Why did the crook take a bath before he robbed the bank? He wanted to make a clean getaway!

How do you throw a party in outer space? You planet.

It's hard to explain puns to kleptomaniacs because they take everything literally.

Parallel lines have so much in common. It's a shame they'll never meet.

Why did dad have to take a break from hauling shellfish? Because he pulled a mussel!

To the person who stole my place in line; I'm after you now.

Why did the house go to the doctor?
It was having window panes.

What do you call a belt with a watch on it?
A waist of time.

Somebody stole all my lamps.
I couldn't be more de-lighted!

I was excited to hear Apple might start making cars until I learned they wouldn't support windows.

Why is grass so dangerous? Because it's full of blades.

SERVER: "Sorry about your wait."
DAD: "Are you saying I'm fat?"

Why did dad buy a universal remote? Because it changes everything.

I hated facial hair, but then it grew on me.

What is at the center of gravity?
The letter "V"!

Why did the boy throw a stick of butter out the window?
Because he wanted to see a butterfly!

Why are ducks bad doctors?
Because they're all quacks.

The butcher backed into the meat grinder and got a little behind in his work.

My wife and I had an argument about which vowel is the most important. I won.

Why did the quiz show give away $10,000 plus one banana? They wanted the prize to have appeal.

Did you hear about the man who stole the calendar? He got 12 months.

A book just fell on my head. I only have my shelf to blame.

Did you hear about the popular cemetery? People were just dying to get in there!

Where in the house should you store your liquor? In the alcohall.

What is the hardest part about skydiving? The ground.

What did the mountain climber name his son? Cliff.

What runs around a baseball field but never moves?
A fence.

Where do you go to get small soft drinks?
Minnesota.

What do you call corn that joins the army?
A kernel.

Are snails faster without their shells?
No, they're more sluggish!

What is a monster's favorite dessert?
I scream.

Why did the Dad stay home after eating seafood?
Because he felt a little eel.

What do you call cattle with a sense of humor?
Laughing stock.

Why does Humpty Dumpty love autumn?
Because Humpty Dumpty had a great fall.

I sold our vacuum cleaner. It was just gathering dust.

Why are elevator jokes so good? Because they work on so many levels.

I asked the IT guy, "How do you make a motherboard?" He said, "I tell her about my job."

It takes guts to be an organ donor.

What do you call a hippie wife?
A Mississippi.

Of all the inventions of the last 100 years, the whiteboard has to be the most remarkable.

What do you call a man who murders breakfast food?
A cereal killer.

Someone stole my mood ring yesterday.
I still don't know how I feel about it.

Why was the baby in Egypt? It was looking for its mummy.

What did one elevator say to the other elevator? I think I'm coming down with something!

I stayed up all night and tried to figure out where the sun was. Then it dawned on me.

How do you find the diameter of a dessert? Use pi.

Why did the cow break up with her boyfriend?
She needed to moove on.

What's another name for a clever duck?
Wise quacker!

How do you deal with fear of speed bumps?
You slowly get over it.

Why can't your hand be 12 inches long?
Because then it would be a foot.

What do you call a shoe made of banana?
A slipper.

What do you get when you cross an elephant with a fish?
Swimming trunks.

How did Darth Vader know what Luke Skywalker got him for his birthday?
He felt his presents.

What's the easiest way to burn 1,000 calories?
Leave the pizza in the oven.

Why did the coffee call the police?
Because it got mugged.

The other day, my wife asked me to pass her lipstick, but I accidentally passed her a glue stick. She still isn't talking to me.

If a rabbit raced a cabbage, which would win?
The cabbage because it's a head.

What did one nut say as he chased another?
"I'm a cashew!"

I searched for a lighter on Amazon, but all I could find were 6,000 matches.

What is more peculiar then watching a catfish? Watching a goldfish bowl.

Son: "Hold on, I have something in my shoe."
Dad: "I'm pretty sure it's a foot."

I'm on a seafood diet. I see food and I eat it.

No matter how much you push the envelope, it'll still be stationery.

What do you call an ant that has been shunned by his community?
Socially dist-ant.

Did you hear about the campsite that was visited by Bigfoot?
It got in tents.

What kind of award did the dentist win?
A little plaque!

What kind of dog does Dracula have?
A bloodhound.

How did the fish plead in court?
Gill-ty.

Why didn't the skeleton go to the dance?
Because it had no body to go with!

Why is no one friends with Dracula?
He's a pain in the neck!

I'll tell you what often gets overlooked; garden fences.

Why do scuba divers fall backward into the water? Because if they fell forward they'd still be in the boat.

The past, the present, and the future walked into a bar. It was tense.

What room does a ghost not need? A living room.

What do you get when you cross a snowman with a vampire?
Frostbite!

Ghosts are bad liars because you can see right through them.

How can you tell a vampire has a cold?
They start coffin.

What do you get when you divide the circumference of a jack-o-lantern by its diameter?
Pumpkin Pi!

How do you fix a cracked pumpkin?
A pumpkin patch.

What is a witch's favorite subject in school?
Spelling.

Do you know where you can get chicken broth in bulk?
The stock market.

What music frightens balloons?
Pop music!

How do you make the number one disappear? You add a "g" and it's "gone".

I asked my date to meet me at the gym, but he never showed up. I guess the two of us aren't going to work out.

A jumper cable walks into a bar. The bartender says, "I'll serve you, but don't start anything."

Someone told me that I should write a book. I said, "That's a novel concept."

What did Venus say to Saturn? "Give me a ring sometime!"

What do you call a dad joke when it gets old? A grandpa joke.

When you ask a dad if he's alright. "No, I'm half left."

Thanks for explaining the word "many" to me... it means a lot.

What do you call a fish with two knees?
A two-knee fish!

What did the buffalo say to his little boy when he dropped him off at school?
Bison.

Did you know that crocodiles can grow up to 15 feet?
But most only have four.

Why is a dad joke like a broken pencil?
Because it has no point.

Where does Bruce Wayne go to use the toilet?
To the batroom.

If I ever find the doctor who screwed up my limb replacement surgery, I'll grab him with my bear hands!

What do you call a factory that makes products that are just average?
A satisfactory.

Angel: "We need to save all the animals from the flood!"
God: "I Noah guy."

I wish I could clean mirrors for a living. It's just something I can see myself doing.

Why did the girl smear peanut butter on the road?
To go with the traffic jam.

Which side of the turkey has the most feathers?
The outside.

On Thanksgiving Day, why did the turkey cross the table?
To get to the other sides.

Justice is a dish best-served cold. If it were warm, it would be just water.

I startled my next door neighbor with my new power tool. I had to calm him down by saying, "Don't worry, this is just a drill!"

I'm reading a horror story in Braille. Something bad is going to happen. I can just feel it.

Why did the bullet end up losing his job? He got fired.

Broken guitar for sale, no strings attached.

My boss told me he was going to fire the person with the worst posture. I have a hunch – it might be me.

Did you hear about the man who fell into an upholstery machine? He's fully recovered.

Why are spiders so smart? They can find everything on the web.

What do you call a cow with no legs?
Ground beef.

Where should you go in the room if you're feeling cold?
The corner- they're usually 90 degrees.

I was a bookkeeper for 10 years.
The local librarians weren't too happy about it.

You used to be able to get air for free at gas stations, but now it costs $1.
That's inflation for you.

74

What did the plate say to the napkin?
"Dinner is on me."

Why do pirates not know the alphabet?
They always get stuck at "C".

What did the bald man say when he received a comb for a present?
"Thanks, I'll never part with it."

I know a guy who collected candy canes.
They were all in mint condition.

> I have kleptomania, but when it gets bad, I take something for it.

> We're renovating the house, and the first floor is going great, but the second floor is another story.

> Not to brag, but I made six figures last year. I was also named the worst employee at the toy factory.

> I talk to myself because sometimes I just need expert advice.

What did one snowman say to another?
Do you smell carrots?

Why was Santa's tiny helper feeling depressed?
Because he had low elf-esteem.

What did Adam say on the 24th of December?
It's Christmas, Eve.

Why did Mrs. Claus buy a lot of spices?
Because she heard Santa Claus is cumin to town.

I quit the art class. It was a little too sketchy.

How does a penguin build its house? Igloos it together.

What falls in winter but never gets hurt? Snow.

My wife asked me to go get 6 cans of Sprite from the grocery store. I realized when I got home that I had picked 7 up.

I only seem to get sick on weekdays. I must have a weekend immune system.

What do you call a sleeping bull?
A bulldozer.

I asked my dad what his New Year's resolution was.
He said, "1920x1080".

What do you call a lonely cheese?
Provolone.

How did the pirate get his ship for so cheap?
It was on sail.

Why was the mathbook sad?
Because it had too many problems.

Two artists had an art contest.
It ended in a draw.

Why don't oysters give to charity?
They're shellfish.

What do you call a dinosaur with an extensive vocabulary? A thesaurus.

There's only one thing I can't deal with, and that's a deck of cards glued together.

How do you make a tissue dance? You put a little boogey in it.

I only know 25 letters of the alphabet, I don't know y.

NURSE: "Blood type?"
DAD: "Red."

Why do cows wear bells? Because their horns don't work.

I started a band called "1023 Megabytes." We haven't gotten a gig yet.

What's the best way to watch a fly-fishing tournament? Live stream.

I once had a dream I was floating in an ocean of orange soda. It was more of a fanta sea.

I thought the dryer was shrinking my clothes. Turns out it was the refrigerator all along.

What did one toilet say to the other? You look flushed.

What are the strongest days of the week? Saturday and Sunday. All the others are weak days.

What do you call a man with a rubber toe? Roberto.

Why do dogs float in water? Because they are good buoys.

Why don't ants get sick? Because they have tiny ant-i-bodies.

Why do frogs never park illegally? They are afraid of getting toad.

Why did the chicken cross the playground?
To get to the other slide.

Can February March?
No, but April May!

When does a joke become a dad joke?
When it becomes apparent.

I told a chemistry joke, but there was no reaction.

What did the janitor say when he jumped out of the closet?
"Supplies!"

What concert costs just 45 cents?
50 Cent featuring Nickelback!

Why did the bicycle fall over?
It was two-tired.

What is the definition of a balanced diet?
A beer in each hand.

What's a caterpillar's favorite swimming stroke?
The butterfly.

What kind of car does a sheep like to drive?
A lamborghini.

What do you call a fish with no eye?
A fsh.

Son: "Dad, can you put my shoes on?"
Dad: "No, I don't think they'll fit me."

87

What did one hat say to the other? Stay here! I'm going on ahead.

I had a happy childhood. My dad used to put me in tires and roll me down hills. Those were Goodyears.

What did the horse say after it tripped? "Help! I've fallen and I can't giddyup!"

Why is Peter Pan always flying? He neverlands.

Wanna hear a joke about paper? Never mind— it's tearable.

Why did the tomato turn red? Because it saw the salad dressing!

What's the best kind of music to listen to when fishing? Something catchy.

Why did the gym close down? It just didn't work out.

How do you make 7 even?
Take away the s.

Why did the politician break up with his girlfriend?
Because he wanted to start seeing other parties!

What do you call it when a snowman throws a tantrum?
A meltdown.

How many tickles does it take to make an octopus laugh?
Ten tickles.

I asked my dad for his best joke and he said, "You."

My dad told me a joke about boxing. I guess I missed the punch line.

What kind of shoes do ninjas wear? Sneakers!

Why do cows have hooves instead of feet? Because they lactose.

When two vegans get in an argument, is it still called a beef?

I'm afraid for the calendar. Its days are numbered.

My wife said I should do lunges to stay in shape. That would be a big step forward.

Singing in the shower is fun until you get soap in your mouth. Then it's a soap opera.

What kind of deer make great weather forecasters?
Rain-deer.

How do you follow Will Smith in the snow?
You follow the fresh prints.

If April showers bring May flowers, what do May flowers bring?
Pilgrims.

How does a taco say grace?
Lettuce pray.

When I heard that Spring is here, I got so excited I wet my plants!

Did you hear about the guy who invented the knock-knock joke? He won the 'no-bell' prize.

What does a sprinter eat before a race? Nothing, they fast!

What do you call an elephant that doesn't matter? An irrelephant.

What did Baby Corn say to Mama Corn? "Where's Pop Corn?"

What's the best thing about Switzerland? I don't know, but the flag is a big plus.

Where do fruits go on vacation? Pear-is!

Why is Yoda such a good gardener? He has green thumbs.

95

What does a lemon say when it answers the phone?
"Yellow!"

What do you call a fish wearing a bowtie?
Sofishticated.

What do you call a pony with a sore throat?
A little hoarse.

Where do math teachers go on vacation?
Times Square

Whenever I try to eat healthy, a chocolate bar looks at me and Snickers.

What does garlic do when it gets hot? It takes its cloves off.

Why do birds fly south for the winter? It's too far to walk!

What's a robot's favorite snack? Computer chips.

What do clouds wear?
Thunderwear.

Why are piggy banks so wise?
They're filled with common cents.

The bank keeps calling me to give me compliments.
They say I have an "outstanding balance."

How do you get a squirrel to like you?
Act like a nut.

What is the Easter bunny's favorite type of music?
Hip-hop.

What's the difference between a hippo and a Zippo?
One is really heavy, and the other is a little lighter.

I don't trust stairs. They're always up to something.

What did the duck say after he finished dinner?
"Put it on my bill."

Did you hear the rumor about butter? Well, I'm not going to spread it!

What do you call a snail on a ship?
A snailor.

What writing utensil does a boar use in class?
A pig pen.

How do you stop a bull from charging?
Cancel its credit card.

How much does a pirate pay to get his ears pierced?
A buck an ear.

Why did the man run around the bed?
He was trying to catch up on his sleep.

How do lawyers say goodbye?
"We'll be suing ya!"

I lost 25% of my roof last night...oof.

What kind of car does an egg drive?
A yolkswagen.

Dad, can you put the cat out?
I didn't know it was on fire.

What do you call an angry carrot?
A steamed veggie.

What do you call cheese that isn't yours?
Nacho cheese.

What time did the man go to the dentist?
Tooth hurt-y.

What's the difference between the bird flu and the swine flu?
One requires tweetment and the other an oinkment.

What kind of key is used to open bananas?
A mon-key.

What did the sushi say to the other sushi?
"Wasabi?"

Why did the sun go to school?
To get brighter!

What does a bee use to brush its hair?
A honeycomb!

Who keeps the ocean floor clean?
Mer-maids.

I used to run a dating service for chickens, but I was struggling to make hens meet.

Why are volcanoes so popular?
They are lava-able.

How did Harry Potter get down the hill?
Walking. JK! Rowling.

If a child refuses to nap, are they guilty of resisting a rest?

What does a cow read every day?
The moos-paper.

Why don't ghosts like the rain? It dampens their spirits.

Why didn't the teddy bear come down for dinner? He was already stuffed.

Did you know corduroy pillows are in style? They're making headlines.

Why do we tell actors to "break a leg"? Because every play has a cast.

I used to play piano by ear.
Now I use my hands.

I once got fired from a canned juice company. Apparently I couldn't concentrate.

A cheeseburger walks into a bar. The bartender says, "Sorry, we don't serve food here."

Have you ever tried to catch fog?
I tried yesterday but I mist.

3.14 percent of sailors are pi-rates.

Why did the scarecrow win an award? Because he was outstanding in his field.

I'm reading a book about anti-gravity. It's impossible to put down!

What did one candy bar say to the other candy bar? "I've got some Twix up my sleeve."

What has hands but can't clap?
A clock.

I was wondering why the frisbee kept getting bigger and bigger.
Then it hit me.

Why did the computer go to the doctor?
It had a virus.

I had a neck brace fitted years ago and I've never looked back since.

You know, people say they pick their nose, but I feel like I was just born with mine.

Why don't cats like walking in the rain?
They are afraid of Poodles.

Why can't you hear a psychiatrist using the bathroom?
Because the 'P' is silent.

What do you get from a pampered cow?
Spoiled milk.

I like telling dad jokes. Sometimes he laughs!

What's the best smelling insect? A deodor-ant.

Where do pens come from? Pennsylvania.

My uncle named his dogs Timex and Rolex. They're his watch dogs.

111

A bartender broke up with her boyfriend, but he kept asking her for another shot.

Did you hear about the guy whose left side was cut off? He's all right now.

If Whole Foods sells sliced apples, Is it false advertising?

I'm an expert at picking leaves and heating them in water. It's my special tea.

I'm so good at sleeping, I can do it with my eyes closed!

What kind of exercise do lazy people do? Diddly-squats.

What do you call a pile of cats? A meowtain.

Two sheep walk into a— baaaa.

I once wrote a song about a tortilla, but it's more of a wrap.

How does the man in the moon get his hair cut?
Eclipse it.

What's Forrest Gump's password?
1forrest1

Dogs can't operate MRI machines.
But catscan.

What does a nosey pepper do?
It gets jalapeño business.

Why do flags always look tired?
Because they're always waving!

What does a pickle say when he wants to play cards?
Dill me in!

What do you call a dad who falls through the ice?
A pop-sicle.

How do you talk to a giant? You use big words!

Which state has the most streets? Rhode Island.

How many telemarketers does it take to change a light bulb? Only one, but he has to do it during dinner.

Why don't seagulls fly by the bay? They'd be bagels.

I could tell you a joke about pizza, but it's a little cheesy.

What did the seal with one fin say to the shark?
If seal is broken, do not consume.

How do you measure the mass of an influencer's following?
By Instagrams!

What do you call a parade of rabbits hopping backwards?
A receding hare-line.

I used to be a personal trainer. Then I gave my too weak notice.

My New Year's resolution is to stop procrastinating. But I will wait until tomorrow to start.

What's the difference between a person's wallet before and after kids? There are pictures where the money used to be.

Why was the computer cold? Because it left its Windows open.

How do you teach kids about taxes? Eat 38% of their ice cream.

My kid is blaming me for ruining their birthday. That's ridiculous, I didn't even know it was today!

My kid gave me a 'World's Best Dad' mug. At least she inherited my sense of humor.

I wish my gray hair started in Las Vegas because what happens in Vegas, stays in Vegas.

What's orange and sounds like a parrot?
A carrot.

Why did the banana go out with the prune?
Because it couldn't get a date.

I wish my kids weren't offended by my Frozen jokes. They really need to let it go!

Why was the broom late for school? It over-swept.

Apparently, you can't use "beef stew" as a password. It's not stroganoff.

What happened when the blue ship and the red ship collided at sea? Their crews were marooned.

What do you call a line of men waiting to get haircuts? A barberqueue.

Where do walls meet after work? The corner.

What vegetable is cool, but not that cool?
Radish.

Where do hamburgers go dancing?
They go to the meat-ball.

How did the cell phone ask his girlfriend to marry him?
He gave her a ring.

What do farmers wear under their shirt when they're cold?
A har-vest.

Which season do people get injured the most?
The fall.

Why did the drum take a nap?
It was beat.

Why did the banker quit his job?
He lost interest!

Why can't a leopard hide?
He's always spotted.

How do you keep a bagel from running away?
You put lox on it.

What do you call a cow in an earthquake?
A milkshake!

Did you hear about the claustrophobic astronaut?
He just wanted a bit more space.

Why did the orange lose the race?
It ran out of juice.

Why did the man fall down the well?
Because he couldn't see that well!

Why are fish so smart?
Because they live in schools!

Why do peppers make such good archers?
Because they habanero.

Where do polar bears store their money?
The snow bank.

How do you keep a bagel from running away?
You put lox on it.

What do you call a cow in an earthquake?
A milkshake!

Did you hear about the claustrophobic astronaut?
He just wanted a bit more space.

Why did the orange lose the race?
It ran out of juice.

Why did the man fall down the well?
Because he couldn't see that well!

Why are fish so smart?
Because they live in schools!

Why do peppers make such good archers?
Because they habanero.

Where do polar bears store their money?
The snow bank.

Where do boats go when they're sick?
To the dock.

What has ears but cannot hear?
A cornfield!

How do trees access the internet?
They log in!

Why don't pirates take baths?
They prefer to wash up on shore.

I was going to look for my missing watch, but I didn't have the time.

What do you call a pencil with two erasers? Pointless.

Did you hear the one about the roof? Never mind, it's over your head.

What do lawyers wear to court? Lawsuits.

What's the weatherman's favorite food in winter?
Brrr-itos!

They say that 3/2 people are bad at fractions.

What did the plumber say to the singer?
Nice pipes.

If the early bird gets the worm, I'll sleep in until there's pancakes.

I ordered a chicken and an egg online. I'll let you know.

I'd avoid the sushi if I were you. It's a little fishy!

What do houses wear? An address.

What did the two pieces of bread say on their wedding day? It was loaf at first sight.

Did you hear about the circus fire? It was in tents.

What did the lightbulb say to his girlfriend? "I love you a watt."

What body of water is the most detail oriented? The Pacific.

What did the grape say when it got stepped on? Nothing, it just let out a little wine.

Made in United States
Orlando, FL
13 June 2024